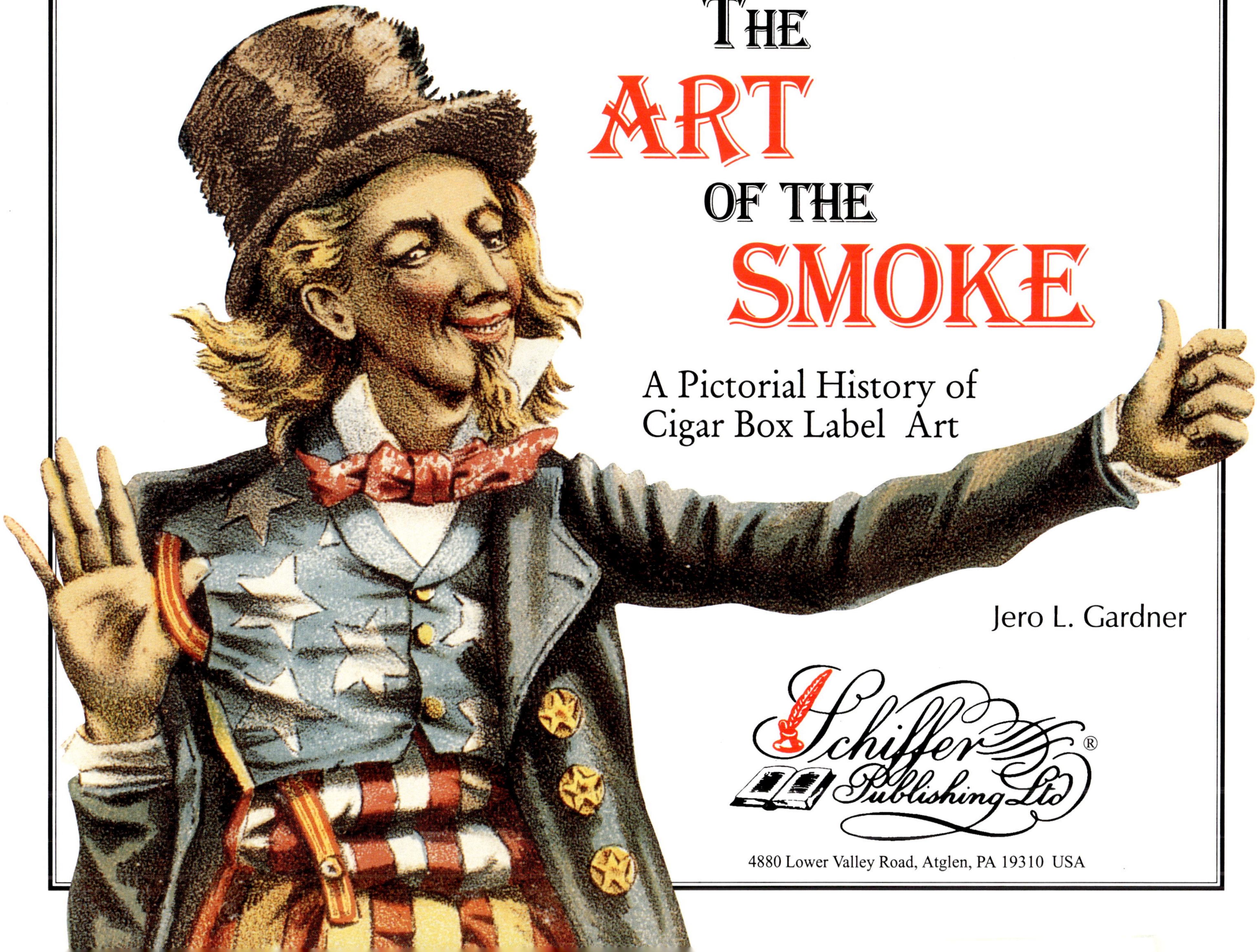

The ART of the SMOKE

A Pictorial History of Cigar Box Label Art

Jero L. Gardner

Schiffer Publishing Ltd®

4880 Lower Valley Road, Atglen, PA 19310 USA

DEDICATION

To my wife, Carol, who never huffed, when I puffed.

Library of Congress Catalog Card Number: 98-85791

Designed by Blair Loughrey
Typeset in Algerian/Zapf Humanist BT

ISBN: 0-7643-0630-8
Printed in China

Published by Schiffer Publishing Ltd.
4880 Lower Valley Road
Atglen, PA 19310
Phone: (610) 593-1777; Fax: (610) 593-2002
e-mail: schifferbk@aol.com
Please write for a free catalog.
This book may be purchased from the publisher.
Please include $3.95 for shipping.

In Europe, Schiffer books are distributed by
Bushwood Books
6 Marksbury Avenue
Kew Gardens
Surrey TW9 4JF England
Phone: 44 (0)181 392-8585; Fax: 44 (0)181 392-9876
e-mail: bushwd@aol.com

Please try your bookstore first.

We are interested in hearing from authors
with book ideas on related subjects.

CONTENTS

INTRODUCTION

What do they say? "A picture is worth a thousand words." No truer statement can be made for what cigar box label art did for the sales of cigars from the mid-1800s through the 1930s.

Thousands of attempts by printers and lithographers to offer fantasy, periodic, political, glamorous, and whimsical art work to cigar-makers prevailed during that period of time when hundreds of cigar-makers were attempting to sell their product to the public. Alas! One of the first marketing and advertising medias began.

Cigar smoking during this period was socially acceptable and, from the male point of view, a part of every day life. From the drawing rooms, front porches, and saloons to the posh mens' clubs and the offices of wanabee financiers, cigar smoking prevailed.

Ah ha! How do we get them to buy our's? Enter the cigar box label, which by the way replaced the plain wooden box that had been hot-branded in a broken letter name or logo, smudged with too much handling.

Busty women, impish children, political figures, sports icons, fastidious gentlemen of means, authors, composers, statesmen, actors, actresses, singers, industrialists, landmark pieces of real estate, quips, double-meaning sayings, gilt, glitz, color, banners, Uncle Sam, and the good old U.S. of A., made up only a part of the lengths printers and lithographers would go to so their labels would be bought and used to grab attention to potential cigar buyers.

Let me tell you that any cigar-maker would change his label as often as we change our underwear. Therefore, the deluge of labels was uncontrollable. By the same token the old labels, or the ones that didn't do the trick, were thrown out or destroyed.

Being a cigar smoker of some forty years, my fascination with cigar labels started early on. Of course, I was much younger then, and scouring antiques dealers and flea markets at the break of dawn was second nature to my desire to collect what I believed to be one of America's first mass marketing advertising pieces.

The Art of the Smoke shows some of the finest examples of cigar box label art and the imagination and creativity of printers and lithographers of the period, who by the way through their creativity are certainly responsible for what you are about to see—early art work, advertising genius at its best.

Oh, and, by the way, if you enjoy a good cigar, light up, sit back, and let yourself wander through the museum of yesteryear's cigar art work. It will never happen again.

In the Beginning—the Early Days

1

Early labels lacked color embossing techniques. The colors were muted and, in many cases, were monochromatic. Many early labels bore the origin of the tobacco, and the names of the plantation and manufacturer. They claimed endorsements of quality and sometimes the "amistad" number (the ship that carried the tobacco to its destination). Not much creativity, but an overture to what was to come.

Figaro. Weise Litho. $575.

Blank Label. $500.

Plantation workers. Weise Litho. $600.

Fabrica de Tobacos.
Esquisitos. $500.

Sea Nymph.
Johns & Co.
$400.

Invitation. Johns & Co. $450.

La Simpatia. Johns & Co. $400.

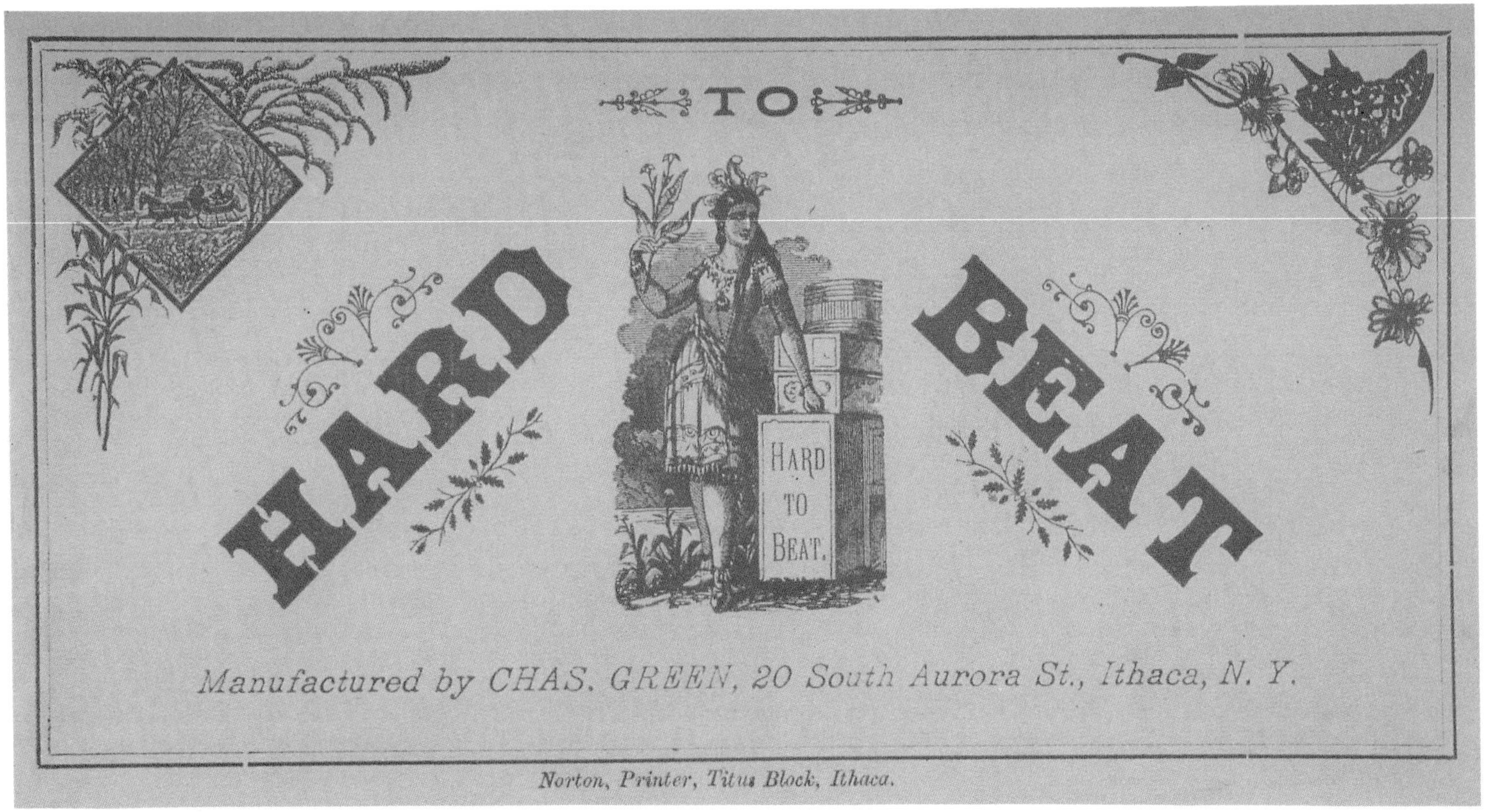

Hard to Beat. Local label printed by Norton, Ithaca, N.Y. $550.

Rich and Rare. Weise Litho. $450.

Jessie. $400.

No. 615. $400.

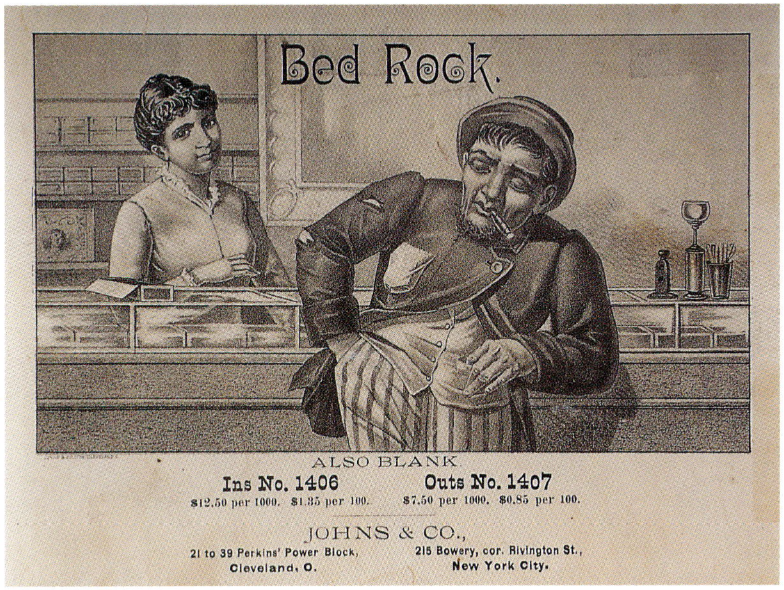

Bed Rock. Johns & Co. $500.

Little Rose. Weise Litho. $400.

Select Me. Weise Litho. $550.

Our Gem. No. 324. Al Weise. $400.

La Flor de Espana. $400.

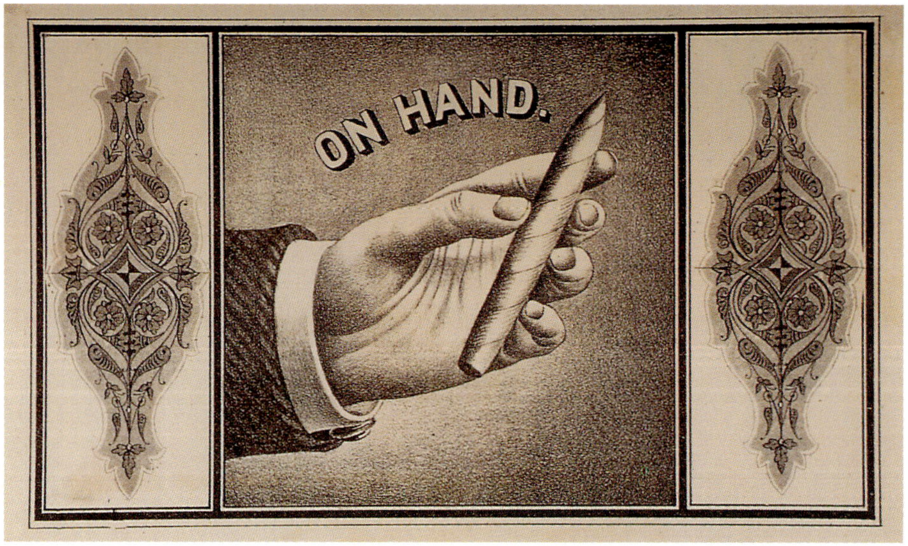

On Hand. Weise Litho. $500.

Cherubs. No.728. $350.

Lovely. $400.

M. Valley Ca.
$400.

Woman touching ears. No. 617. $400.

Eagle. Weise Litho. $400.

Noblesse Oblige. Weise Litho. $450.

La Ele Gancia. Weise Litho. $450.

The Trade Cigar. $400.

The Herald. Johns & Co. $350.

Woman in the woods. No. 700. $400.

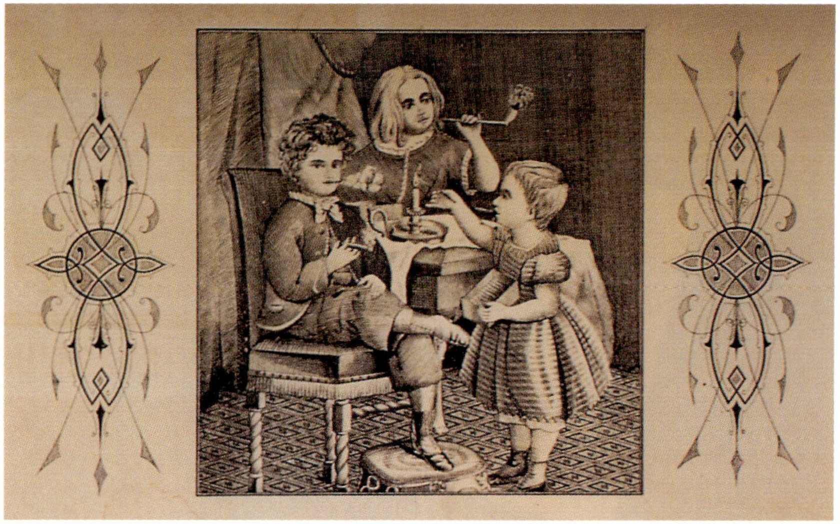

Children smoking'. Weise Litho. $450.

Tantalizers. $400.

Daisy. Geo. Harris & Sons. $500.

No name. Litho. by Witsch & Schmidt, N.Y. $500.

Left: Captivator. Weise Litho. No. 732. $500.

Below left: Our Proclamation. Litho. by Witsch & Schmidt, N.Y. $500.

Below: Loreley. Weise Litho. $500.

"Old Style." Johns & Co. $450.

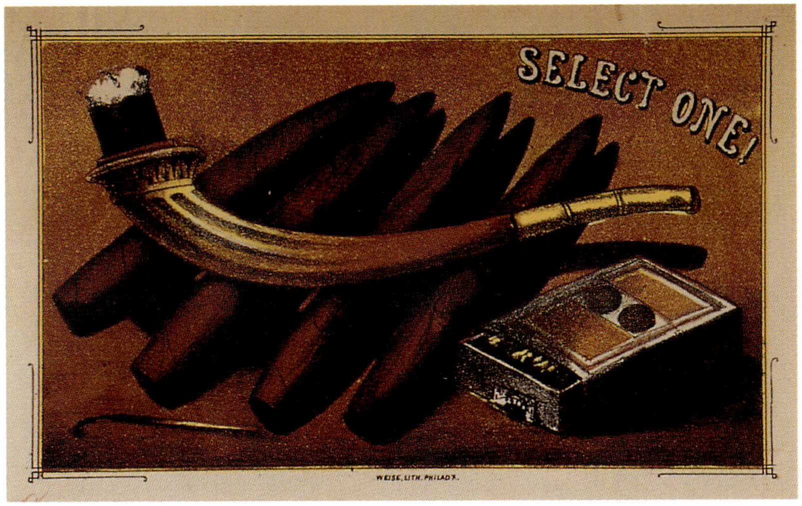

Select One. No. 544. Weise Litho. $600.

Flora Fina. E. Steffens Litho. $475.

Blue Bird. $500.

Arrow. No. 752. $500.

Jolly Jokers. Johns & Co. $500.

Fives. Johns & Co. $500.

The Latest. Johns & Co. $500.

Pocket-Pieces. O. L. Schwencke, N.Y. $500.

Drummers Pride. Johns & Co. $500.

Elsie. $475.

You Know. $800.

Sampling. Johns & Co. $800.

It's All In the Design

2

Design was the theme, and usually showed up in elaborate and geometric borders, leaving the centers for the creative copy writers—as you will see.

Habana. No. 545. Weise Litho. $550.

A Muriasy Ca. Habana.
Weise Litho. No. 308. $500.

Conchas. No. 372. Weise Litho. $500

F. Garcia & Bros. 1900. $375.

Blank label. $400.

Oasis blank. Johns & Co. $300.

Manuel Garcia Alonso. $300.

Banner with foilage. Johns & Co. $300.

Blank with lion. No. 1428. Johns & Co. $300.

Persian blank. No. 1382. Johns & Co. $300.

Blank label. F. M. Howell & Co. $300.

Blank label. Howell & Co. $300.

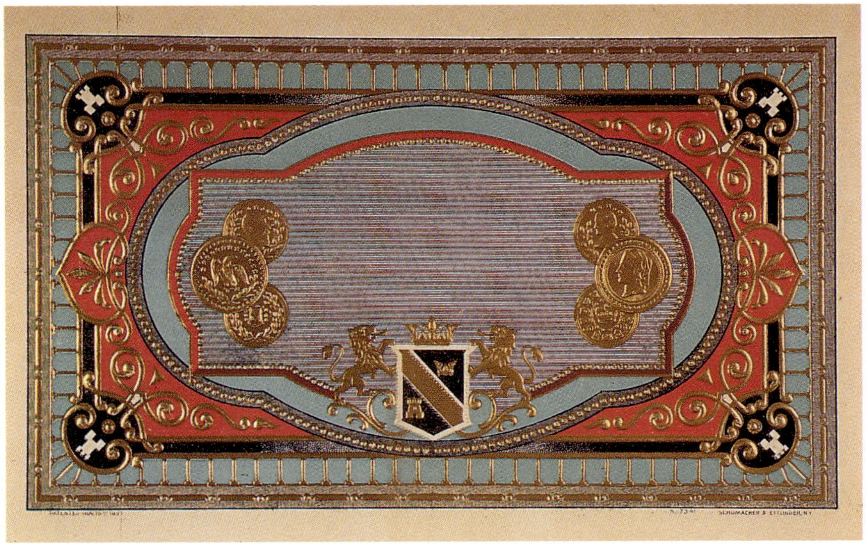

Blank label. Schumacher & Ettlinger, N.Y. $300.

Blank label. 1897. Schmidt & Co. $300.

Blank label. $500.

Blank label. $450.

3 Prim and Proper Manners, It's the Sign of the Times

Curtsy, bow, kiss the back of her hand. Cinched waists, stuffed shirts, handle-bar mustaches, spooning, and calling cards were the signs of the times. Permission, a must, to court the lovely lady—but no permissions needed to enjoy a fine cigar. Oh well!

Club Friends. 1896. Schmidt & Co. $900.

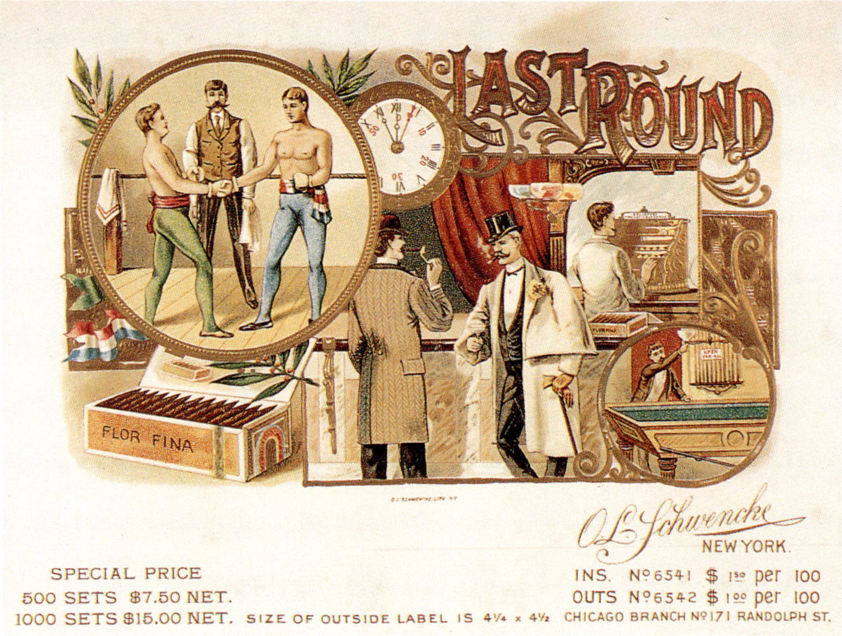

Last Round. O.L. Schwencke, N.Y. $600.

Gentlemen of Quality. $700.

Turnover Club. H. E. Ackerburg. $850.

Our Club Rooms. Geo. S. Harris & Sons Lith., Phila. $700.

Jolly Bachelor.
$800.

Gold Prize. $500.

Home Comfort. Johns & Co. $500.

Zip. Johns & Co.
$500.

Social Smoke.
O. L. Schwencke,
N.Y. $700.

Early Days. No. 3077.
Moehle. $450.

Top left: My Favorite. O. L. Schwencke, N.Y. $500.

Top right: The Flirt. Calvert Litho. Co. $500.

Lower left: First Blush. $500.

Lower right: Belvedere. Schmidt & Co. $500.

Pastime. O. L. Schwencke, N.Y. $500.

Ever True. O. L. Schwencke, N.Y. $500.

Opera. O. L. Schwencke, N.Y. $500.

Cuban Cigars. Schmidt & Co. $500.

Left: Your Treat. O. L. Schwencke, N.Y. $500.

Lower left: The Gem. Geo. Harris & Sons. $900.

Lower right: High Toned. O. L. Schwencke, N.Y. $900.

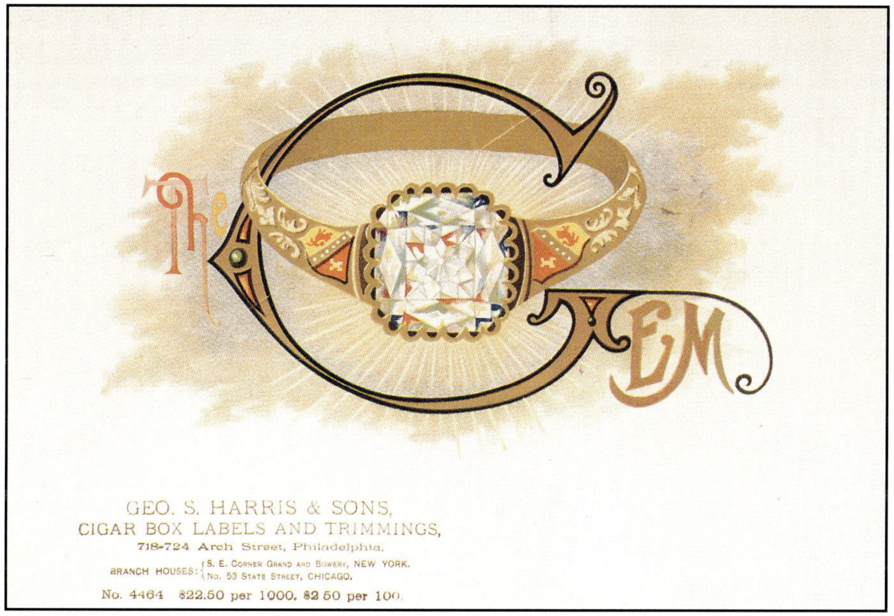

Left: Flirt. 1897. Schmidt & Co. $1000.

Below left: Compliments of the Season. $700.

Below right: Compliments of the Season. $700.

Compliments of the Season. 1905 American Litho. $700.

Merry Christmas. Krueger & Braun. New York. $600.

Beneficio. Schumacher & Ettlinger. $600.

Birthday. Schumacher & Ettlinger. $600.

La Molesta. $400.

Home Lights. $500.

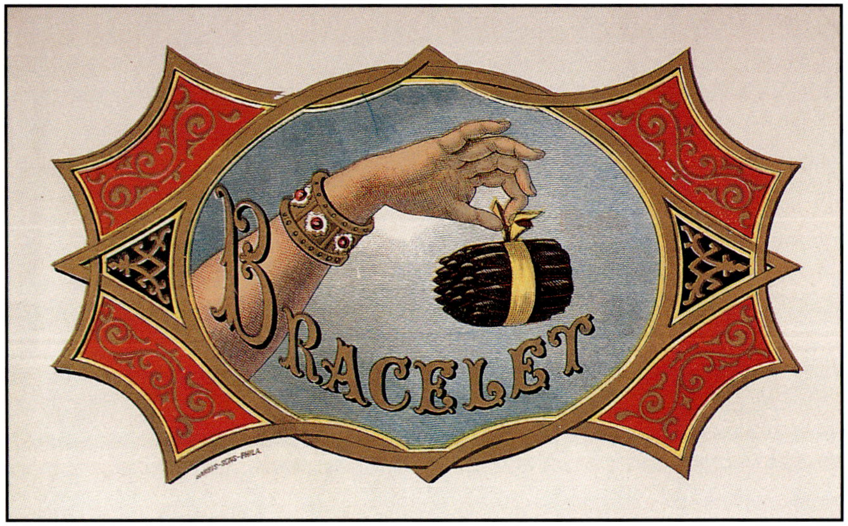

Bracelet. Harris & Sons. $500.

Merry Makers. Schumacher & Ettlinger. $600.

Lavish Ladies and a Bounty of Beauties

4

Well here they are! Ladies, gals, girls, women from the stage, and some that left on the last stage. Singers, temptresses, exotics, and considering the times a few erotics. Buttoned up or cleavage showing, these beauties certainly did their fair share to get those *seegars* sold.

Nanon. Johns & Co. $300.

Top left: Rose Bride. Schmidt & Co. $500.

Top right: Edna. 1897. Schmidt & Co. $450.

Left: Belinda. $450.

Lillian Russell. $450.

Lilly. $500.

Floss. $500.

Sweet Flowers. 1896. Schmidt & Co. $500.

Society Belle. $450.

Red Cap. O. L. Schwencke, N.Y. $450.

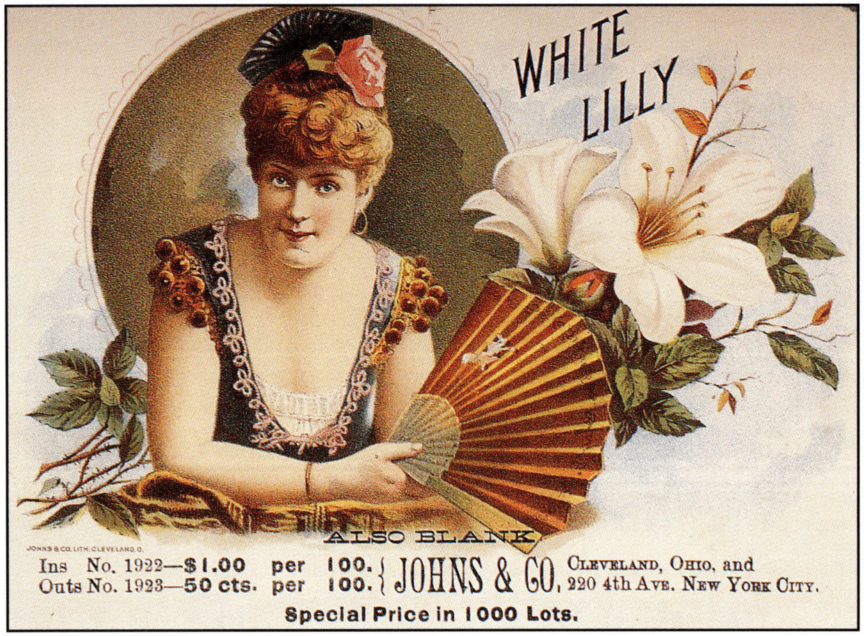

White Lilly. Johns & Co. $450.

La Gloria de Cuba. O. L. Schwencke, N.Y. $400.

Above left: Golden Star. O. L. Schwencke, N.Y. $450.

Above right: Best Five. Weise Litho. $600.

Right: Patience. No. 734. $500.

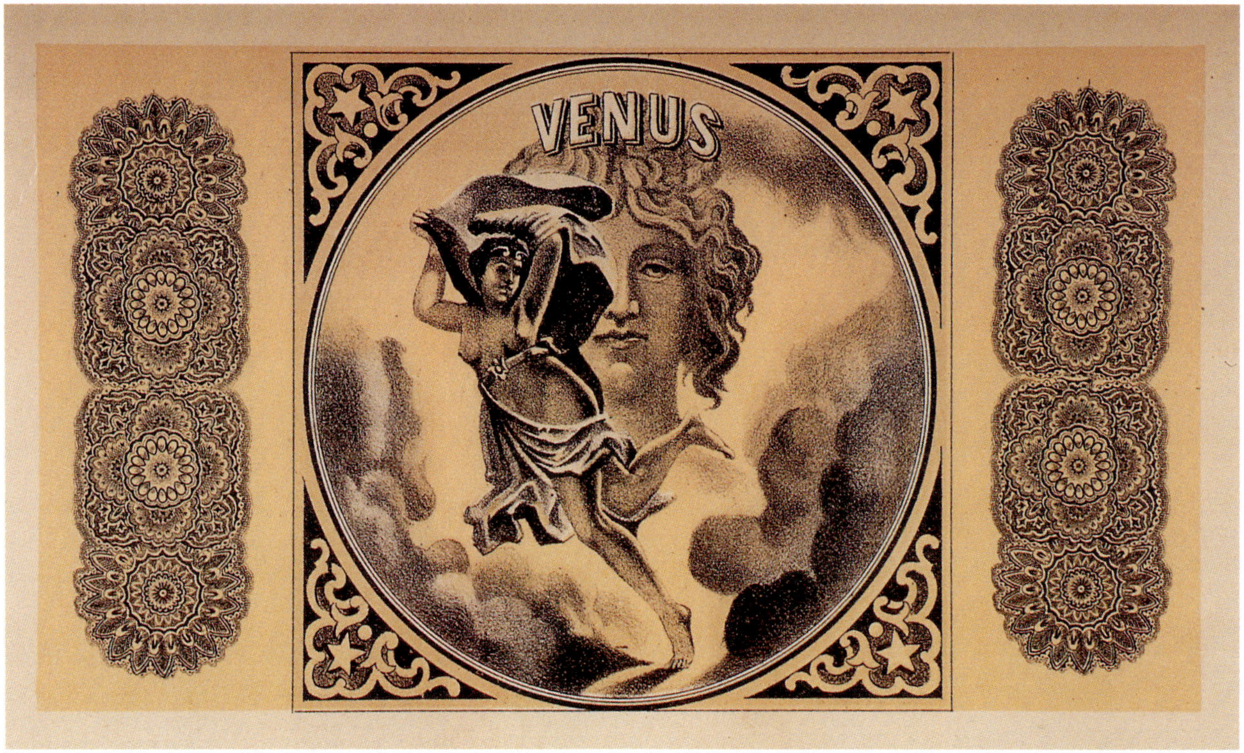

Venus. Weise Litho. $475.

La Muna. $400.

Gran Fabrica de Tabacos Puro's. $450.

Donna Roma. $400.

Favorite. O. L. Schwencke, N.Y. $500.

Pine Burr. O. L. Schwencke, N.Y. $450.

Golden Belle. O. L. Schwencke, N.Y. $450.

Lady Flash. O. L. Schwencke, N.Y. $500.

Vienna Beauties. Consolidated Litho. $450.

Lu Lu. $450.

Jano. $475.

La Carolina. $450.

La Clarina. 1902. American Litho. $400.

Astra Bella.
$450.

Top left: Blank label. Merz & Son. $450.

Top right: Snap Shot. 1925. J. A. McDoo, Charlotte, N.C. $500.

Left: Key West Beauty. O. L. Schwencke, N.Y. $450.

Violets. 1896. Schmidt & Co. $500.

Ondina. $400.

Baby Rose. No. 977. 1912. Moehle. $500.

Sweet Violet. Austin, Nichols & Co. Inc. $450.

Elaine. Schmidt & Co. $450.

Nefta. $450.

Priscilla. $400.

Top left: Madame Butterfly. $500.

Top right: Victoria Noblessa. Litho. Geo. Schlegel. $400.

Right: Golden Web. O. L. Schwencke, N. Y. $700.

Seidenzahl's Neola. Gustav. A. Otto. $400.

Lillian Ashley. $500.

Marie Antoinette. $400.

Baxter. Bobrow Bros., Phila. $400.

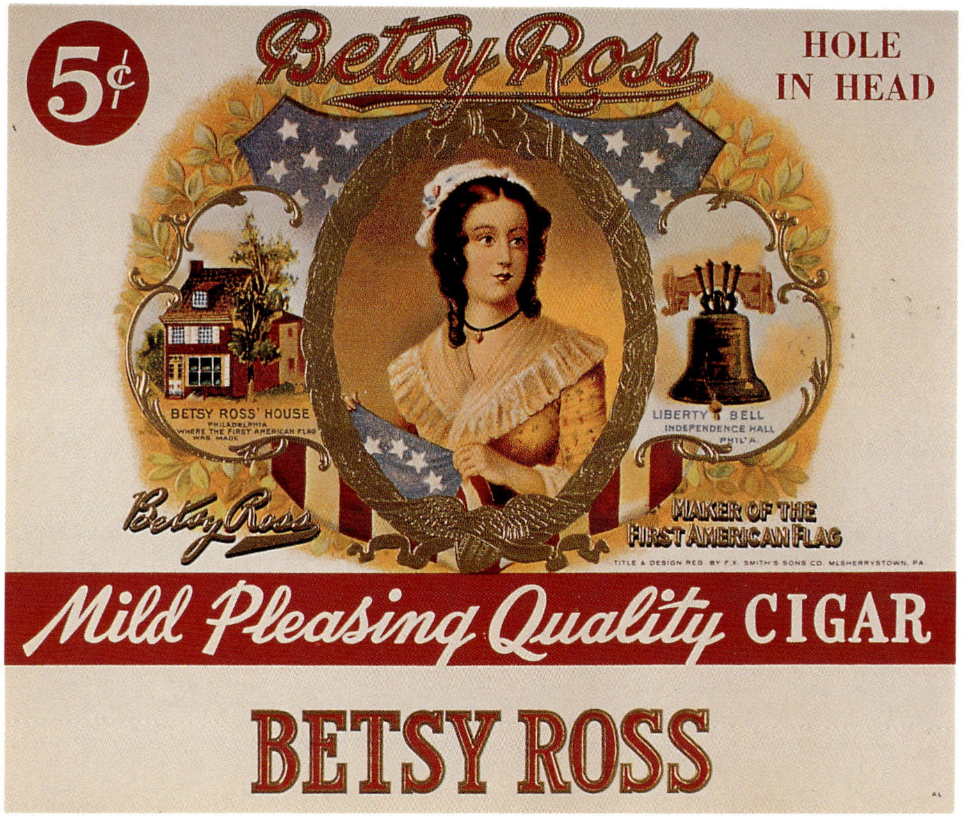

Right: Betsy Ross. $700.

Bottom left: Ozama. $400.

Bottom right: Florence Walton. $400.

Polly. Johns & Co. $300.

Blank label. $400.

Peggy O'Neal. $400.

Santa Fe. $400.

Above: Wedding Bells. $500.

Right: Ysidora. $700.

Left: Brand New. 1897 Schmidt & Co. $650.

Bottom left: Goldie. No. 3055. 1917. Moehle. $475.

Bottom right: Katy Barry. $400.

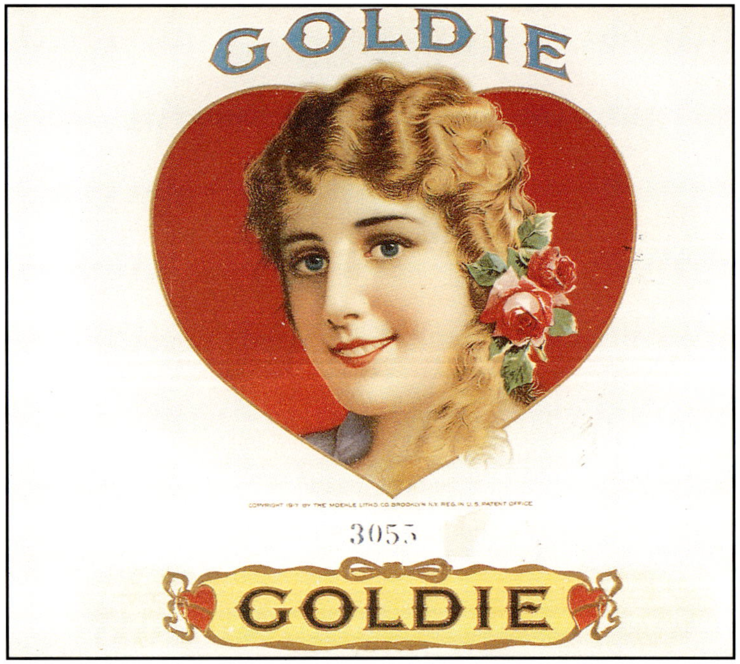

Left: Daizee. American Litho. $600.

Bottom left: Julia Marlowe. $400.

Bottom right: Lady Churchill. $400.

Men, the Famous and the Infamous

5

Politicians, presidents, big shots, and bullies; literary leaders, bankers, and commercial icons are only a few. On stage or off, when it came to "puffers," the men ruled the roost.

Muhlenberg. Litho. Geo. Schlegel, N.Y. $800.

Happy Felix. $500.

National Speaker. Consolidated Litho. $800.

Henry W. Longfellow. P. R. C. Co. $800.

Hamilton Fish. $800.

Judge Taft. $800.

Lord Curzon. Sulzberger-Oppenheimer Co. Ltd. $700.

Senator Dixon. $700.

Right: Austin Blair. $800.

Bottom left: William Bond. O. L. Schwencke, N.Y. $450.

Bottom right: Little Victor. O. L. Schwencke, N.Y. $400.

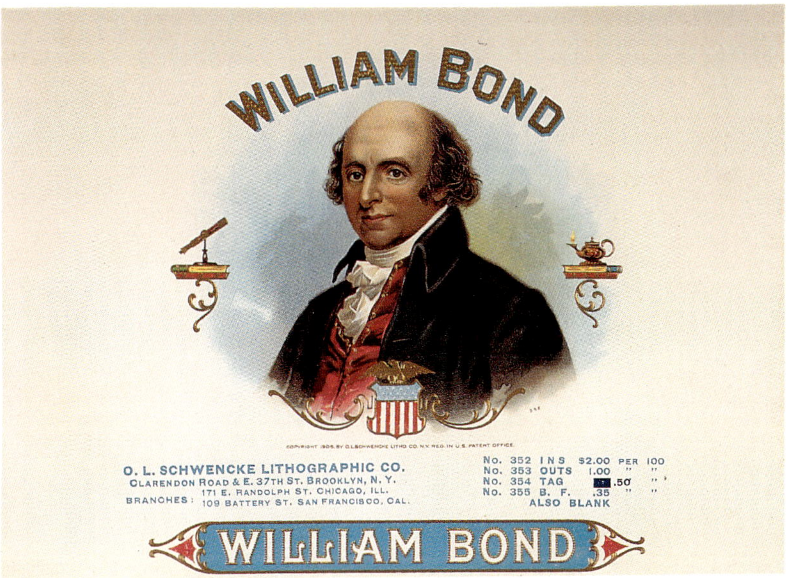

Left: Knight of Pythias. O. L. Schwencke, N.Y. $500.

Bottom left: Invicta. Geo. Schlegel. $500.

Bottom right: Sherlock Holmes. $800.

Pulaski. Consolidated Litho. $500.

Bryant. 1899. Schmidt & Co. $800.

Astor. Hull Grummond & Co. Inc. $1000.

Baron Munchausen. 1896. Wm. Wicke Co. $900.

Cuba Libre. 1897 W. W. Co. $600.

Duke of Coburg. $700.

H. S. Northrup. $850.

Andy Gump. $900.

Round. $700.

Shamrocks. Litho. Geo. Schlegel, N.Y. $800.

Flor de Rothenberg. $700.

John B. Stetson. $700.

James Kent. $700.

Tom Moore. $700.

Dick Custer. $800.

Old Abe. $800.

Above: William the Fourth. $1000.

Left: Nabob. Calvert Litho. $600.

General Hartranft. 1899. Consolidated Litho. $800.

The Senator. $550.

Joe Cannon. Consolidated Litho. $800.

Cable Cabinet. Cyrus Field, Chandler White, S.F.B. Morse, Moses Tayolor, Marshallo Roberts, Peter Cooper, D. D. Field. $800.

Top left: Farragut. Calvert Litho. $900.

Top right: The Finest. O.L. Schwencke, N.Y. $600.

Right: Real Judge. No. 750. $600.

Delaware. Washington's army crossing the Delaware, Dec. 26, 1776. Consolidated Litho. $600.

Old Rounder. O. L. Schwencke, N.Y. $575.

Old Judge. O. L. Schwencke, N.Y. $700.

Partner. American Lithographic Co. N.Y. $700.

Left: Tanory's Best Fina. American Litho. $700.

Bottom left: Irish Singer. $700.

Bottom right: Enrico Caruso. Consolidated Litho. $800.

Top left: Rudolph Valentino. $900.

Top right: Lord Macaulay. $700.

Right: Tannhauser. $800.

Right: Andrew Mack. Litho Geo. Schlegel, N.Y. $700.

Below: L. J. S. $700.

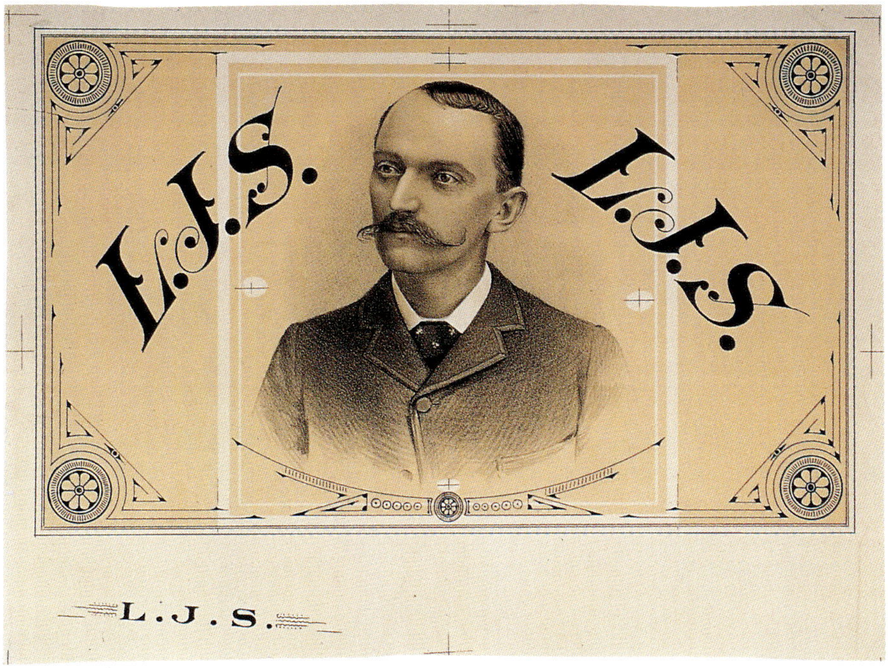

Old Hickory. Consolidated Litho. $700.

Solid Five. O. L. Schwencke, N.Y. $600.

Flor de Shenkberg. $600.

Paul Clay. $800.

James K. Polk. $800.

James Madison. $800.

Steuben. 1876. $800.

Mt. Rushmore. $900.

Flor de Girard. $800.

First Cabinet. Thos. Jefferson, Sec. of State; Hendrick Knox, Sec. of War; John Adams, Vice Pres.; Geo. Washington, President; Alex. Hamilton, Treas. Consolidated Litho. $850.

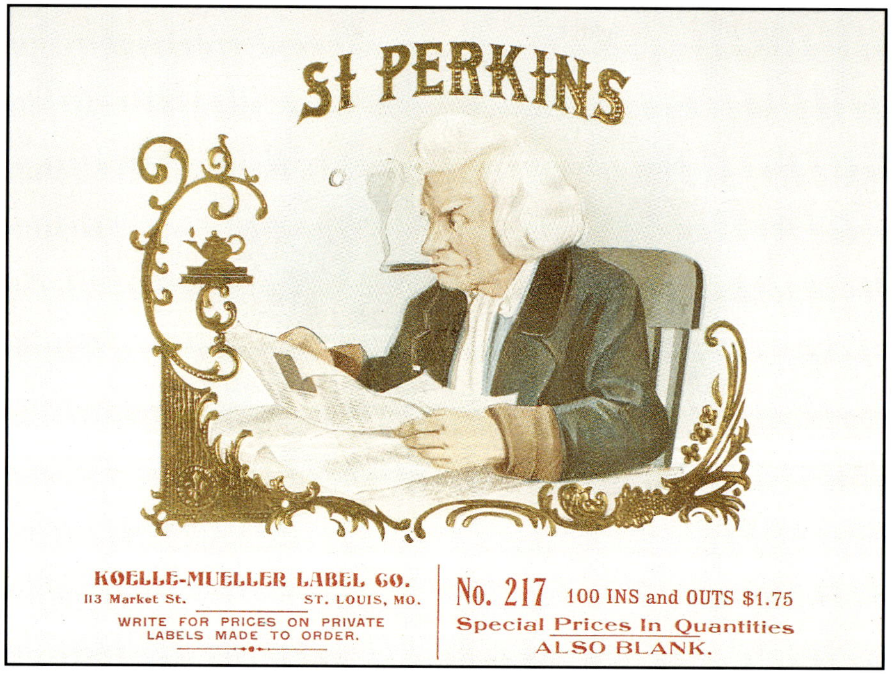

U.S. Supreme Judge. Chief Justice Fuller, Justice Gray, Justice Shiras, Justice Brewer, Justice Lamar, Justice Field, Justice Brown, Justice Blatchford, Justice Harlan. Reg. Nov. 1888. $800.

St. Perkins. Koelle-Mueller Label Co., St. Louis. $500.

Top left: Our Leader. O. L. Schwencke, N.Y. $500.

Top right: Cosi fan Tutti. 1897. Schmidt & Co. $500.

Right: Check. Harris & Sons. $500.

Admiral Fairfax. Louis E. Neuman & Co. $800.

Lucky John. 1911. Moehle. $600.

Robert Bacon. $700.

Flor de Warren. $700.

Rodin. C. B. Henschel Mfg. Co. $450.

Harry Houck. F. M. Howell & Co. Elmira, N. Y. $500.

General Gates. $700.

Our Friend. $800.

Union Leader. O. L. Schwencke, N.Y. $500.

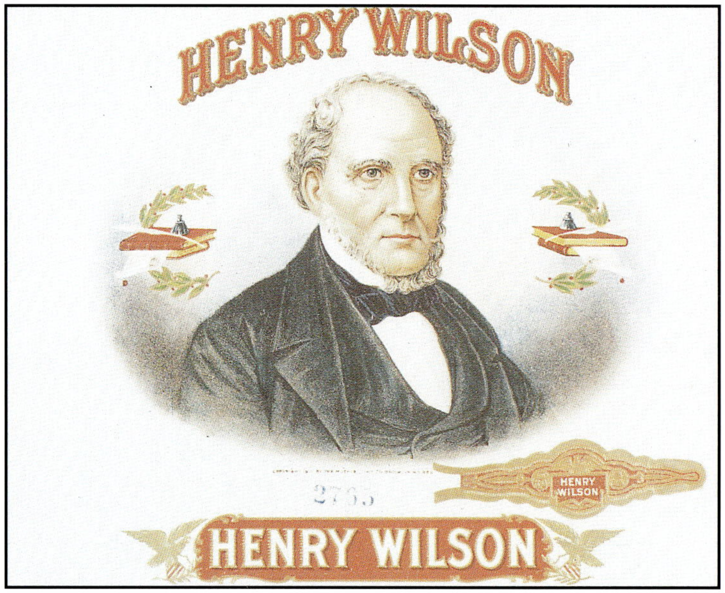

Henry Wilson. 1911. Moehle. $400.

Hoosier Poet. $500.

Lucky Bill. $700.

Stephen Day. $800.

John Deere. Litho. Geo. Schlegel, N.Y. $800.

Calvin S. Brice. $800.

Newcomer. $800.

Izaak Walton. $475.

Richard Peters. First Secretary of War. $500.

Private Secretary. Johns & Co. $600.

Top left: Abe Martin. $400.

Top right: El Adelantado. Johns & Co. $600.

Right: Jupiter. $1000.

Tennyson. $475.

Old Swep. $500.

Ben Austrian. $700.

Uncle Dooley. O. L. Schwencke, N.Y. $800.

Leland Stanford. $800.

La Flor de J. Russell Young. $800.

Edward Parke. $700.

John W. Mackay. A. C. Kaufmann & Co. Makers, N.Y. $800.

6 They're Old, They're Rare, and They're Expensive

The best of the best! Old and very rare, if there were a cigar box label section in the Louvre, these labels would be there. They represent the very finest examples of cigar box label art. Some are so rare that they may be the only ones in existence. So look, but *don't touch!*

Bryan and Stevenson. Schmidt. 1900. $8,500.

Lime Kiln Club. May 22, 1883. $5,000.

The Nations Choice. $4,500.

Fishes. Original artwork. $4,500.

A Light? No 726. $4,000.

Real. Weise Litho. $3,500.

Artists proofs. $3,500.

Top left: De Anselmo. Weise Litho. $3,500.

Top right: Little African. $3,000.

Right: Let's Share. Weise Litho. $3,000.

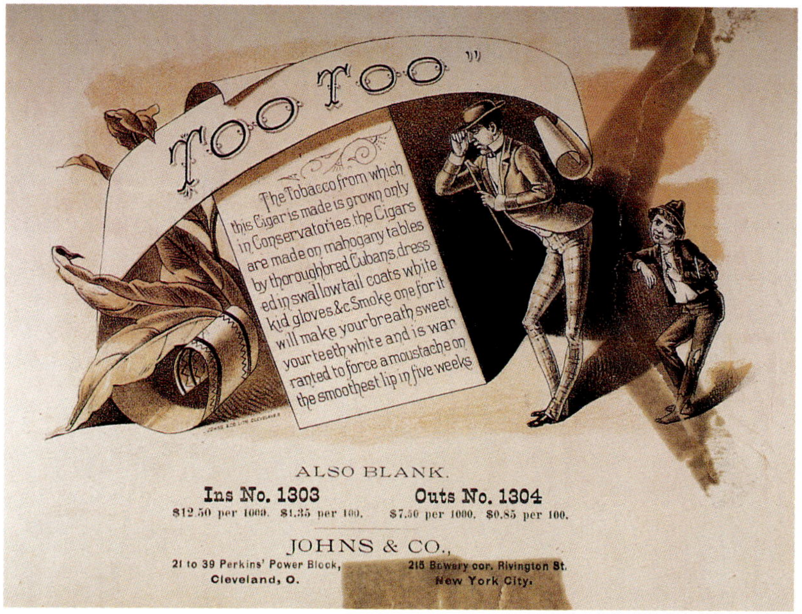

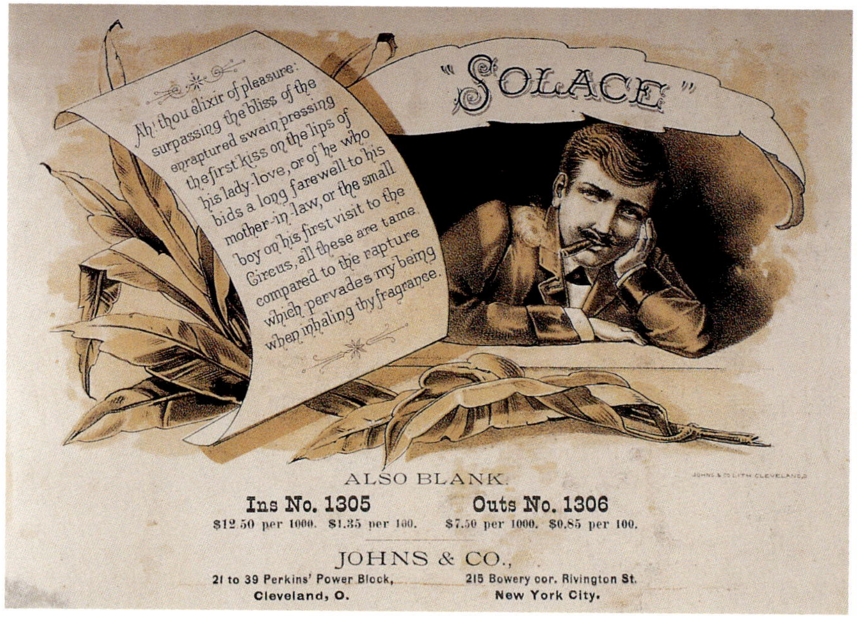

Top left: Too Too. Johns & Co. Cleveland, Ohio and New York. $3,000.

Top right: Solace. Johns & Co. $3,000.

Left: On Deck. Johns & Co. $3,000.

"No Monkeying." Emil Steffens. $3,000.

Top left: Jockey Club. Weise Litho. $2,500.

Top right: Trump. Schmidt & Co. $2,500.

Left: A. Lincoln. $2,500.

Top left: Franklin D. Roosevelt. $2,500.

Top right: Souvenir de Ortmann. $2,000.

Right: Sapristi! $2,000.

Left: American Conquest. 1898. Schmidt & Co. $2,000.

Bottom left: Blank label. 1899. Krueger & Braun. $1,500.

Bottom right: High Toned. $1,500.

Saturn. G. Sharp & Son. Phila. $1,500.

Gesundheit. Johns & Co. $1,500.

Los Inmortales. F. Heppenheimer's Sons. $1,500.

Blank label. $1,500.

Found at Last. Weise Litho. $1,500.

The smoking bull. Weise Litho. $1,500.

Henry Clay. Weise Litho. $1,100.

Left: Lincoln Bouquet. B. Newmark & Co. $1,500.

Bottom left: Extra Fives. 1897. Schmidt & Co. $1,000.

Bottom right: From Farm to Whitehouse. No. 327. Koelle-Mueller Label Co, St. Louis. $1,000.

Right: Gettysburg Commanders. Globe Litho. Co, N.Y. $1,000.

Bottom left: La Flor de Lincoln. $1,000.

Bottom right: Uncle Sam. $1,000.

Above: Falstaff. Heppenheimer's & Sons. $1,000.

Left: Flor de Tabacos. $1,000.

Below: Occident. Weise Litho. $900.

Top left: Flor de Alma. Weise Litho. $900.

Top right: Illinois Giants. Lyman Trumbull, Gen. U. S. Grant, Abraham Lincoln, Gen. John A. Logan, Stephen A. Douglas. Cole Litho. Co., Chicago. $900.

Right: Uncle Dudley. $900.

La Reposa. $900.

Immense. Weise Litho. $900.

Blank label. $900.

Mephisto Cigars. F. Heppenheimer's Sons, N.Y. $900.

Puck. $900.

Scud. Geo. S. Harris & Sons. $900.

Lover's Assistance.
Weise Litho. $900.

7 Plenty of Chiefs and Some Indians

And rightfully so. After all, they came before cigars, and most certainly before cigar box labels.

Chief Okee. 1912. Moehle. $600.

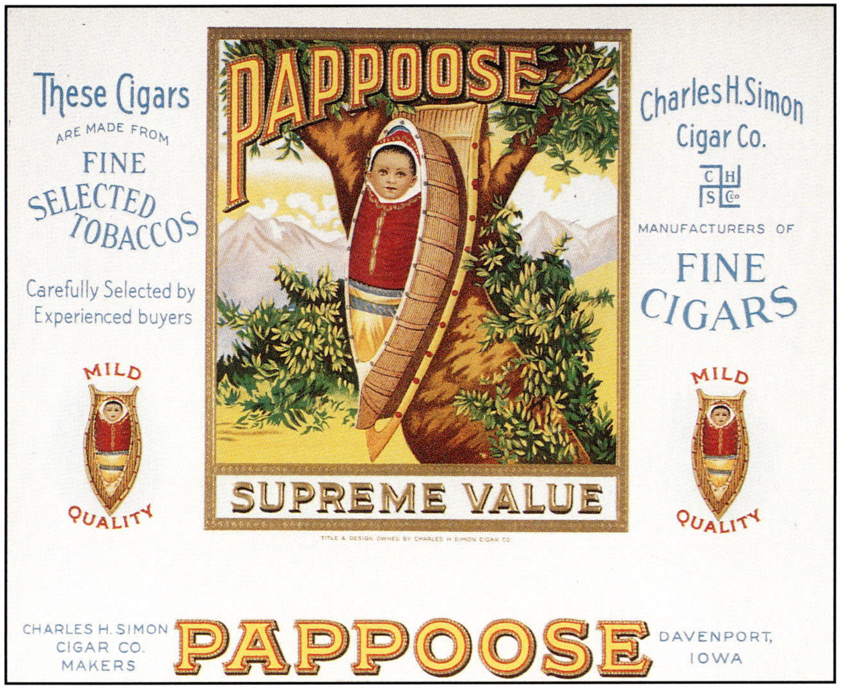

Pappoose. Consolidated Litho. $550.

Red Cloud. $500.

Blank label. $600.

Six Nations. C. F. Lighton & Co. $500.

Left: Chief Joseph. Petre, Schmidt & Bergsman Lith., N.Y. $700.

Bottom left: Chief Fives. Koelle-Mueller Label Co. $600.

Bottom right: Sheboygan. $600.

Mocassin Maid. Geo. Schlegel. $600.

Spearsman. $600.

Red Circle. $600.

American Kid. $600.

Blank label .1903. C. B. Henschel Mfg. Co. $500.

Zena. $600.

Lone Trail. 1901. Schmidt & Co. $800.

Seminola. $600.

Queen of the Straits. Calvert Litho. $600.

Pawnee. $600.

Black Hawk. 1938. H. Fendrich, Inc. $600.

Tonkawa. $600.

Talk From the Animals

8

If "Old McDonald had a farm," then cigar box labels certainly gave a fair share of acknowledgment to animals—the tame, the wild, as well as the birds and the bees.

Bird. No. 604. $300.

Foresters. Johns & Co. $450.

Woodcock. $600.

Cunningham's Pointers. $600.

Stago. $600.

Fox. $600.

Kennel Club. Geo. Schlegel. $800.

White Cat. $700.

Scarlet King. $600.

Right: Attention. F. M. Howell & Co. $800.

Bottom left: Shetland Ponies. $700.

Bottom right: Big Moose Cigar. $700.

Cracker. $700.

Indiana Elk. $600.

Red Snapper. $800.

Monkey Brand. $750.

The Big Baer Cigar. 1903. Schmidt & Co. $500.

Jack. Harris & Sons. $900.

Yellow Hornet.
$700.

White Elephant. $600.

"Our Pointer." O. L. Schwencke, N.Y. $500.

Baby Elephant. No. 658. $500.

Victorious. Weise Litho. $500

Top left: Big Wolf. $600.

Top right: Pug. Schumacher & Ettlinger. $600.

Right: Alcazar. Consolidated Litho. $700.

Black Bass. $600.

Double Bull Head. $600.

Stag Horn. O. L. Schwencke, N.Y. $450.

Big Bear. $600.

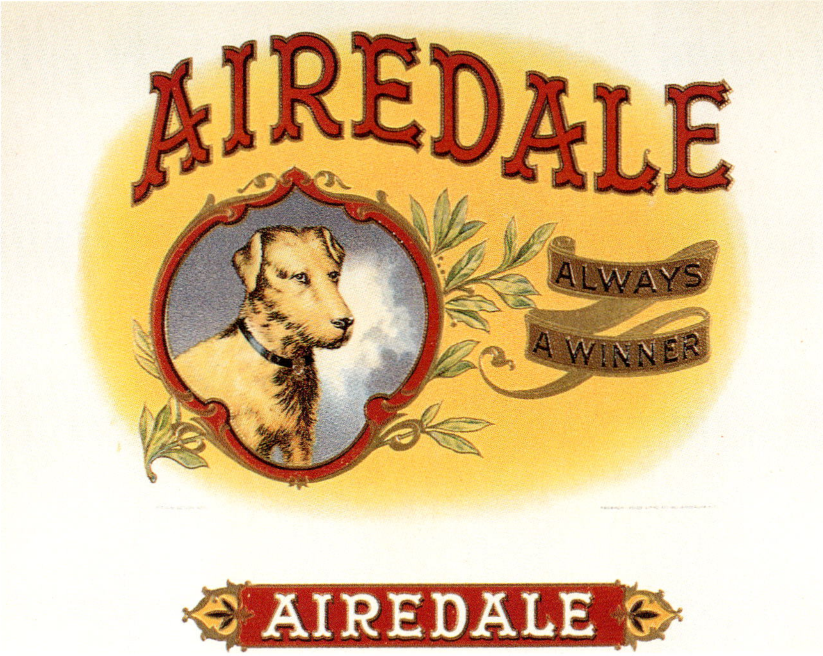

Airedale. Pasbach-Voight Litho. $500.

Above: Stier Head.
1896 Schmidt. $500.

Left: Beeswing. $500.

HONK-HONK! BEEP-BEEP! TOOT-TOOT!

BETTER GET OFF THE TRACKS!

9

Horse and buggy, trains, those wonderful men in their flying machines. Cigar box labels were not limited to people, places, and things, but gave a good chronology of the way people got around and what vehicles they used for travel.

Havana Special. O. L. Schwencke, N.Y. $450.

Navy Pride.
Schmidt & Co.
$500.

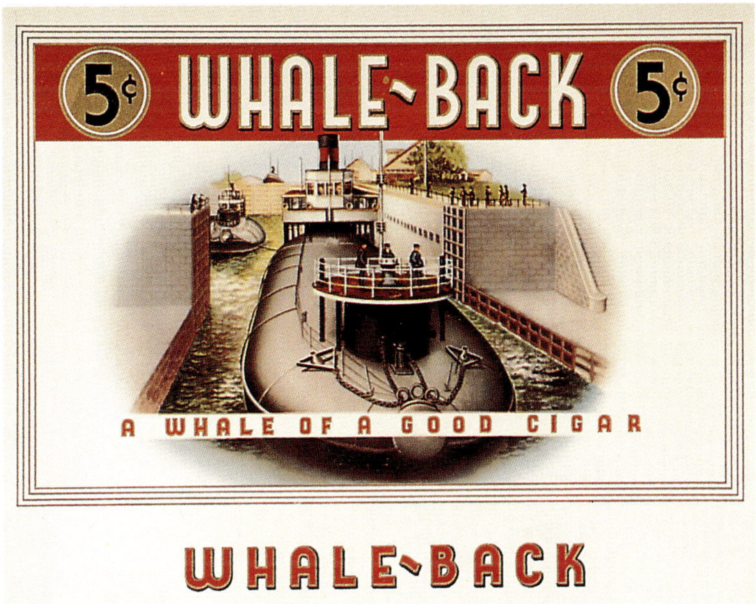

Whale-Back. $600.

Great Southern. $600.

World's Greatest Flyer. $650.

Spirit of St. Louis. American Litho. $650.

Dayton Flyer. $600.

Overland. $600.

Majestic. $700.

Above: Sigari Tripoli. $675.

Right: Our Flyer. O. L. Schwencke, N.Y. $700.

10 Locations! Places! And the Sporting Life!

Location, location, location. We've all heard that, and cigar box labels made sure that those special places, those brick, stone, and steel edifices of Industry and Learning were memorialized on many a box of stogies.

Festina. Weise Litho. $400.

Club House. O. L. Schwencke, N.Y. $600.

Above: Ravisloe Club. $450.

Left: Silver Lake. $400.

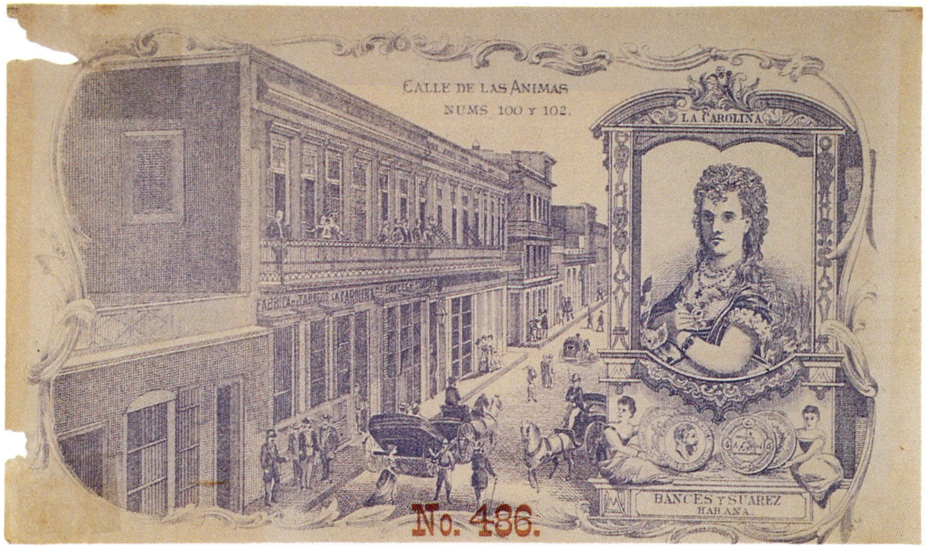

Calle de Las Animals. No. 486. $500.

Flor de Cardenas. Louis E. Neuman & Co. $575.

Windsor Castle. Weise Litho. $350.

The Original Park & Tilford Store. $500.

Diaz Bances Y Co. Weise Litho. $575.

M. Jane (building). Weise Litho. $475.

College Chums. The Model. Photo of Cornell University by McGillivray $500.

Morgan Cigar Co. $400.

Left: Henry Clay. $550.

Bottom left: La Trabugo. $500.

Bottom right: Empire State. $400.

The Iroquois Perfecto. $400.

El Figaro. Weise Litho. $450.

Clinton Hill. Gustav Redmann. $350.

Clifton Park Special. $450.

Birthplace of Daniel Webster. Artist's proof. $500.

Barrena. $575.

Manuel Lopez. $500.

Columbia Dome. $600.

Lady Violet. Hermann Bruns & Son. $500.

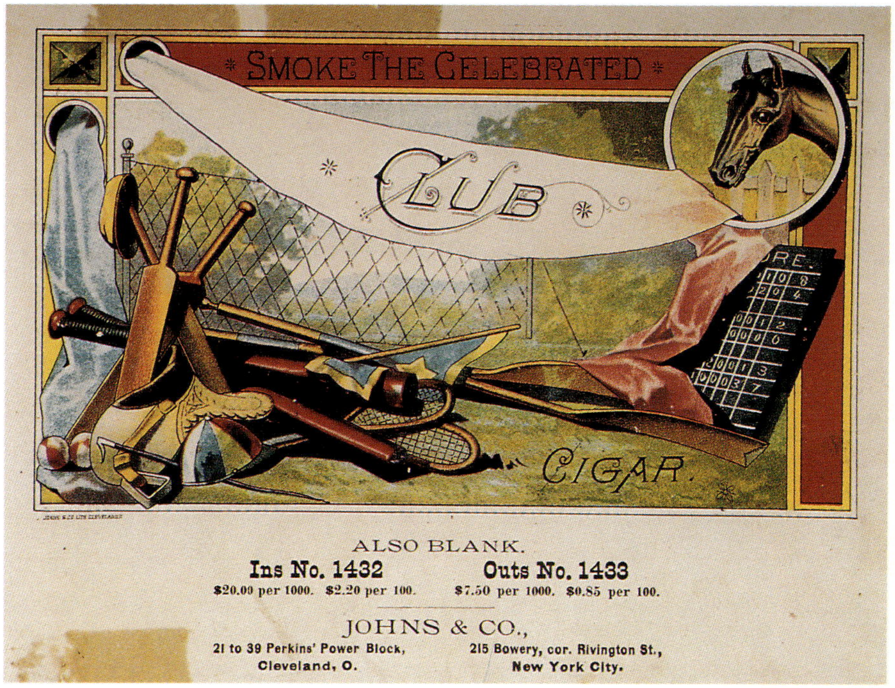

Clug. Johns & Co. $450.

Fine Catch. 1890 Krueger & Braun. $500.

Challenge. Weise Litho. $600.

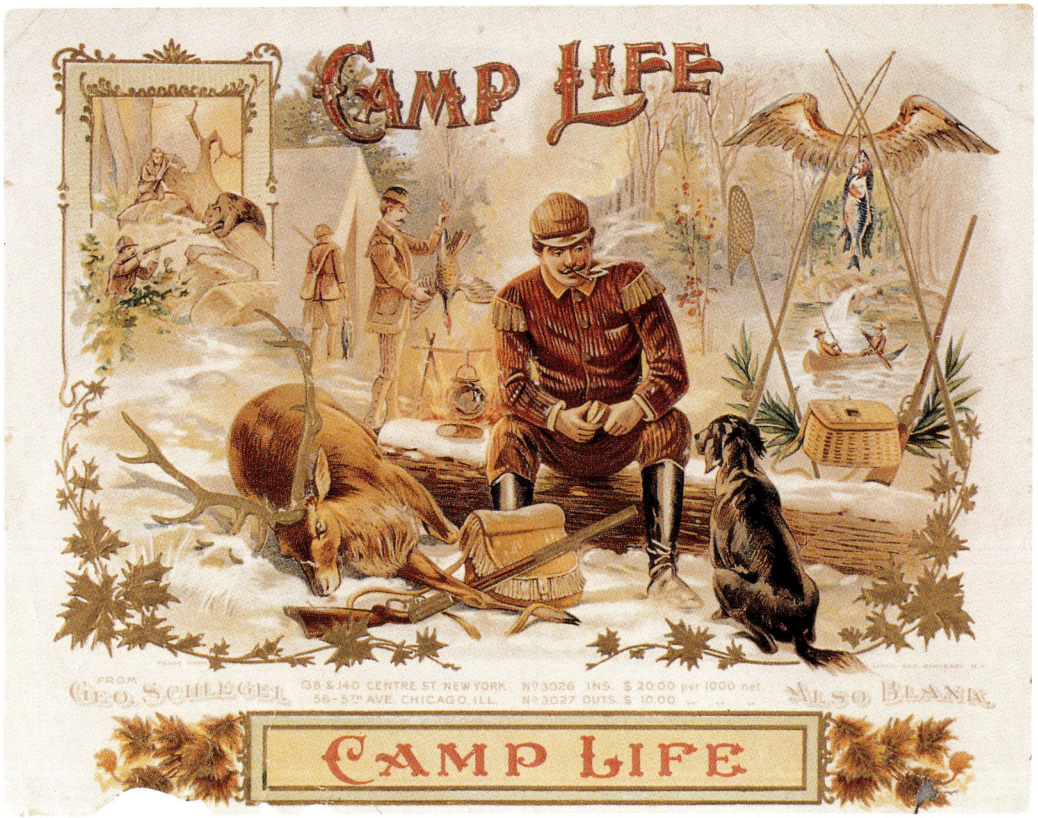

Top left: Good Record. O. L. Schwencke, N.Y. $500.

Top right: County Fair. O. L. Schwencke, N.Y. $600.

Left: Camp Life. Geo. Schlegel. $900.

Great Sport. F. M. Howell & Co. $800.

Camp Fire. 1919. C. B. Henschel. $600.

Sea Side. No. 744. Weise Litho. $500.

Double Header. 1911. Moehle. $575.

Along Shore. O. L. Schwencke, N.Y. $500.

Country Club. W. H. Snyder & Sons. $400.

Blank label. $700.

On Deck. O. L. Schwencke, N.Y. $500.

Frontier. H. B. Grauley. $700.

Above: The Crack Runner.
Louis E. Neuman & Co. $700.

Left: Bowling Club. 1902.
Schmidt & Co. $850.

Top left: Hunter's Reward. 1901. Schmidt & Co. $500.

Top right: First Goal. Krueger & Braun. $600.

Right: Sports. O. L. Schwencke, N.Y. $500.

Phrases, Slogans, and Sayings

11

This was the most prolific time in cigar box label production. Set aside what you see, but listen to what we say! "We're the Best!" "Forget the Rest," "Big Boy," "Take a Few," and "Don't Forget, They're Only 5¢."

Press Club.
$350.

Left: Headlights. O. L. Schwencke, N.Y. $500.

Bottom left: Domestic. O. L. Schwencke, N.Y. $450.

Bottom right: Elegant. O. L. Schwenke, N.Y. $450.

King Highball. $300.

Nicko. Schmidt & Co. $450.

New York Special. O. L. Schwencke, N.Y. $450.

Hard to Beat. O. L. Schwencke, N.Y. $400.

Left: Nickel Boom. Schmidt & Co. $700.

Bottom left: Uncle Willie Cigars. $300.

Bottom right: Honey Suckle. $250.

Charming Stock. Hermann Bruns & Son. $450.

Union Favorite. Moehle. $500.

Spinning Girl. 1896. Geo. Harris & Sons. $400.

Genteel. $350.

Something New. O. L. Schwencke, N.Y. $450.

Morning-Tap Cigar. Seider Cigar Co. $400.

Dutch Maid. $350.

Left: Square Deal. Schmidt & Co. $500

Bottom left: Royal Casket. Geo. S. Harris & Sons. $400.

Bottom right: The Doctor Cigar. $400.

Left: C. B. Christman Brothers. $900.

Bottom left: Engagement. F. X. Smith's Sons Co., McSherrystown, Pa. $600.

Bottom right: Little Scout. $550.

Good Prospects. 1886 Schumacher & Ettlinger, N.Y. $900.

C B Cigar. $800.

8 Hours. Johns & Co. $375.

Resolution. Johns & Co. $450.

So Far, So Good.
Weise Litho.
$550.

Hidden Fortune. $300.

First Medal. No. 677. $400.

Druggist Choice. $400.

Bank Roll. $400.

Union Mark. Schmidt & Co. $450.

Lorna Doone. $450.

Little Cousins. $450.

Swift Runner. $400.

Choice Puff Cigars. $350.

Double S. $300.

Mark of Honor. Schmidt & Co. 1904. $450.

Healthy Stock. Hermann Bruns & Son. $450.

The Stroller Cigar. F. W. Howell & Co., Elmira, New York. $275.

Faultless. O. L. Schwencke, N.Y. $500.

Hi-De-Ho Stogie. $300.

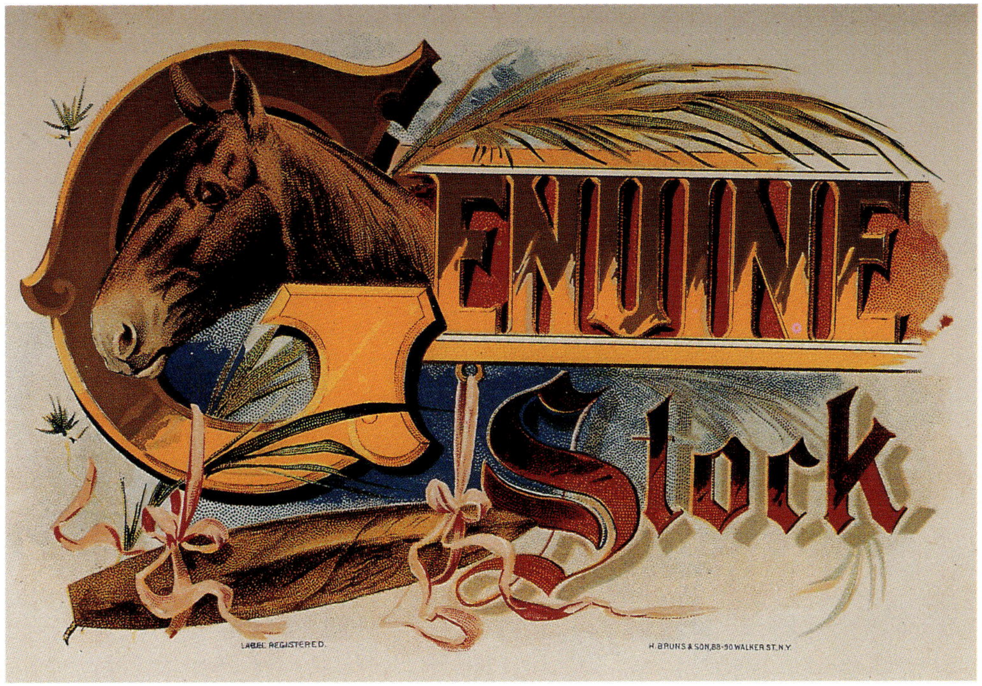

Genuine Stock. Hermann Bruns & Son. $500.

Immense. O. L. Schwencke, N.Y. $500.

Latest Style. O. L. Schwencke, N.Y. $500.

Above: Pleasant Stock. Hermann Bruns & Son. $450.

Top right: Nov. 11th Victory Day. Celestino Fernandez & Co. $700.

Right: Sonny Boy. $700.

Above: Three Twins. $600.

Top right: Fair Exchange. O. L. Schwencke, N.Y. $600.

Right: 1861. Consolidated Litho. $800.

Ultimatum. Globe Litho. Co., N.Y. $800.

Planter's Punch. 1914. Moehle. $500.

Fine Stock. O. L. Schwencke, N.Y. $500.

Crack Cigar. $550.

Who's Kicking! Johns & Co. $800.

Nickel Leaders. Schmidt & Co. $400.

Happy-Medium. $300.

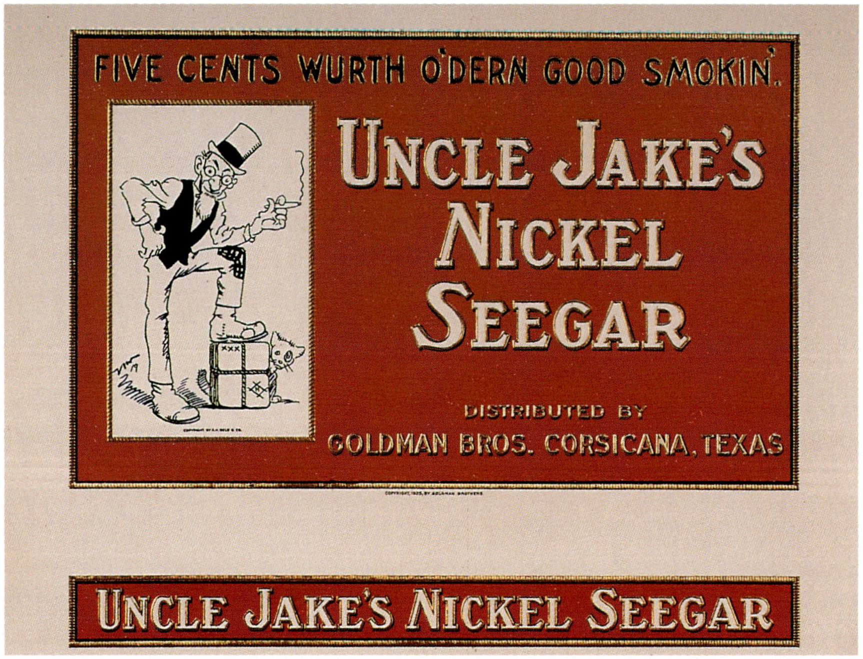

Uncle Jake's Nickel Seegar. 1925. Goldman Bros., Corsicana, Texas. $475.

Illinois Club House. $450.

We Should Worry. Moehle. $450.

New Pleasure. Pleasing Mildness. $500.

Frazzle. American Litho. $500.

White Ash. O. L. Schwencke, N.Y. $500.

Above: Doctor's Special. 1912. Moehle. $450.

Top right: Tourist. A. O. Fisher & Co. $450.

Right: Bill Fold. $500.

Right: Snow Flake. $750.

Bottom left: Special 5. O. L. Schwencke, N.Y. $475.

Bottom right: Navy Fives. $500.

St. Paul Club. $675.

Wizard. $450.

Old Mixon.
$400.